# Ur

**By Iain Gray**

79 Main Street, Newtongrange,
Midlothian EH22 4NA
Tel: 0131 344 0414 Fax: 0845 075 6085
E-mail: info@lang-syne.co.uk
www.langsyneshop.co.uk

Design by Dorothy Meikle
Printed by Printwell Ltd


ISBN 978-1-85217-221-3

# Urquhart

# Urquhart

**SEPT NAMES:**
Cromarty.

**MOTTO:**
Mean weil, speak weil, and do weil.

**CREST:**
A naked woman brandishing a sword in her right hand and a palm sapling in her left.

**TERRITORY:**
Ross-shire, Inverness-shire,
Moray, Aberdeenshire.

*Chapter one:*

# The origins of the clan system

by Rennie McOwan

**The original Scottish clans of the Highlands and the great families of the Lowlands and Borders were gatherings of families, relatives, allies and neighbours for mutual protection against rivals or invaders.**

Scotland experienced invasion from the Vikings, the Romans and English armies from the south. The Norman invasion of what is now England also had an influence on land-holding in Scotland. Some of these invaders stayed on and in time became 'Scottish'.

The word clan derives from the Gaelic language term 'clann', meaning children, and it was first used many centuries ago as communities were formed around tribal lands in glens and mountain fastnesses.

The format of clans changed over the centuries, but at its best the chief and his family held the land on behalf of all, like trustees, and the ordinary clansmen and women believed they had a blood relationship with the founder of their clan.

There were two way duties and obligations. An inadequate chief could be deposed and replaced by someone of greater ability.

Clan people had an immense pride in race. Their relationship with the chief was like adult children to a father and they had a real dignity.

The concept of clanship is very old and a more feudal notion of authority gradually crept in.

Pictland, for instance, was divided into seven principalities ruled by feudal leaders who were the strongest and most charismatic leaders of their particular groups.

By the sixth century the 'British' kingdoms of Strathclyde, Lothian and Celtic Dalriada (Argyll) had emerged and Scotland, as one nation, began to take shape in the time of King Kenneth MacAlpin.

Some chiefs claimed descent from

ancient kings which may not have been accurate in every case.

By the twelfth and thirteenth centuries the clans and families were more strongly brought under the central control of Scottish monarchs.

Lands were awarded and administered more and more under royal favour, yet the power of the area clan chiefs was still very great.

The long wars to ensure Scotland's independence against the expansionist ideas of English monarchs extended the influence of some clans and reduced the lands of others.

Those who supported Scotland's greatest king, Robert the Bruce, were awarded the territories of the families who had opposed his claim to the Scottish throne.

In the Scottish Borders country – the notorious Debatable Lands – the great families built up a ferocious reputation for providing warlike men accustomed to raiding into England and occasionally fighting one another.

Chiefs had the power to dispense justice and to confiscate lands and clan warfare produced a society where martial virtues – courage, hardiness, tenacity – were greatly admired.

Gradually the relationship between the clans and the Crown became strained as Scottish monarchs became more orientated to life in the Lowlands and, on occasion, towards England.

The Highland clans spoke a different language, Gaelic, whereas the language of Lowland Scotland and the court was Scots and in more modern times, English.

Highlanders dressed differently, had different customs, and their wild mountain land sometimes seemed almost foreign to people living in the Lowlands.

It must be emphasised that Gaelic culture was very rich and story-telling, poetry, piping, the clarsach (harp) and other music all flourished and were greatly respected.

Highland culture was different from other parts of Scotland but it was not inferior or less sophisticated.

Central Government, whether in London or Edinburgh, sometimes saw the Gaelic clans as

*"The spirit of the clan means much to thousands of people"*

a challenge to their authority and some sent expeditions into the Highlands and west to crush the power of the Lords of the Isles.

Nevertheless, when the eighteenth century Jacobite Risings came along the cause of the Stuarts was mainly supported by Highland clans.

The word Jacobite comes from the Latin for James – Jacobus. The Jacobites wanted to restore the exiled Stuarts to the throne of Britain.

The monarchies of Scotland and England became one in 1603 when King James VI of Scotland (1st of England) gained the English throne after Queen Elizabeth died.

The Union of Parliaments of Scotland and England, the Treaty of Union, took place in 1707.

Some Highland clans, of course, and Lowland families opposed the Jacobites and supported the incoming Hanoverians.

After the Jacobite cause finally went down at Culloden in 1746 a kind of ethnic cleansing took place. The power of the chiefs was curtailed. Tartan and the pipes were banned in law.

Many emigrated, some because they

wanted to, some because they were evicted by force. In addition, many Highlanders left for the cities of the south to seek work.

Many of the clan lands became home to sheep and deer shooting estates.

But the warlike traditions of the clans and the great Lowland and Border families lived on, with their descendants fighting bravely for freedom in two world wars.

Remember the men from whence you came, says the Gaelic proverb, and to that could be added the role of many heroic women.

The spirit of the clan, of having roots, whether Highland or Lowland, means much to thousands of people.

*Chapter two:*

# Castles and conflict

**Bearers of the surname of Urquhart are scattered widely across the globe today, but what links them in an indissoluble bond is that they can all trace roots back to the ancient soil of the northeast of Scotland.**

While Urquharts flourished for many centuries in Moray and Aberdeenshire, it is in the area of Cromarty, in Ross-shire, and further south in Inverness-shire that they first made their mark on the pages of Scotland's colourful story.

A Gaelic version of the name is Uchardan, believed to indicate 'fort on a knoll', 'by a rowan wood', or 'the front of the knowe', while another derivation is from the Brythonic 'air' and 'cairdean', indicating 'at the woods.'

As a surname, Urquhart is a 'location' name, stemming from the territory known in Gaelic as 'Urchard', or 'Airchartdan', on the scenic northwest shore of Loch Ness, and this indeed was the name of the area as early as the sixth century when visited by the great missionary and future saint, Columba.

There is also an area known as Glenurquhart further northeast, in the Black Isle, however, and there is still debate as to whether or not this was the original homeland of the Urquharts.

What is not in doubt, however, is that both areas became firmly identified with the Urquharts from an early date.

'Mean weil, speak weil, and do weil', (with 'weil' meaning 'well') is the Urquhart motto, while a naked woman brandishing a sword in her right hand and a palm sapling in her left is the crest of this clan that claims as their founder a famed warrior known as Conachar Mor.

Conachar, a son of the Royal House of Ulster, is believed to have come to Scotland from Ireland during the reign from 1058 to 1093 of Malcolm III, better known to posterity as Malcolm Canmore.

A colourful legend associated with

Conachar Mor is that, aided by his faithful hound An Cu Mor, he slew a wild boar that had been terrorising all who lived in the area of the present day Great Glen, and his sword is said to still lie buried somewhere in the glen.

The boar's head that appears in Clan Urquhart's heraldic devices is said to commemorate Conachar's memorable slaying of the boar.

As one of Malcolm Canmore's greatest and most fearless warriors, Conachar is reputed to have been rewarded with possession of the fortress that later became the site of the imposing edifice of Urquhart Castle, on the northwest shore of Loch Ness.

The occupation of the castle by the Urquharts in succeeding centuries appears to have been sporadic however, with Durwards, MacDonalds, and Grants its main occupants.

But the history of the Urquharts is still romantically linked with that of the castle, whose precious ruins are today in the expert care of Historic Scotland.

Situated near Drumnadrochit, Urquhart

Castle is one of Scotland's most popular tourist attractions, and its dramatic history is recounted in an exhibition and audio-visual display in the castle's magnificent new visitor centre.

The ruins also overlook the stretch of Loch Ness that boasts the greatest number of sightings of one of Scotland's other top tourist attractions – the elusive Loch Ness Monster, more fondly known as Nessie!

Built on the site of ancient fortifications around approximately 1200, Urquhart Castle survived centuries of turmoil only to be blown up in 1692 to prevent it becoming an impregnable and strategically important stronghold for dissident northern Jacobites.

An impressive tower house still defiantly stands among the ruins, however, as mute testimony to the past might of what was one of Scotland's largest castles.

One of the most tumultuous periods in the castle's long and bloody history occurred during Scotland's late thirteenth and early fourteenth century War of Independence with England, a period that coincides with the Urquharts' first appearance in the historical record.

This was in the form of William de Urchard, the first chief of the clan, who proved a loyal supporter of the great warrior king Robert the Bruce in his struggle to free Scotland from the yoke of English occupation.

At an early stage in the long and bitter conflict, William de Urchard commanded a hardened band of freedom fighters who prevented supporters of England's rapacious Edward I from seizing the Mote Hill, overlooking the mouth of the Cromarty Firth, thereby denying them access to a strategically important ferry crossing.

Urquhart Castle also held a vital strategic importance and, in common with the other northern bastions of Banff, Elgin, and Inverness castles, changed hands many times before Bruce's decisive victory at the battle of Bannockburn in June of 1314.

This was when a 20,000-strong army under Edward II was defeated by a Scottish army less than half this strength – a patriot army that included William de Urchard and his clansmen.

In 1358, during the reign of David II, William's son, Adam, was rewarded for the family's loyalty to the cause of Scotland's freedom and independence with the award of the hereditary sheriffdom of Cromarty, an influential and powerful post in which the family served with great distinction for 300 years.

As the power and influence of the Urquharts increased and their fortunes flourished, Castle Craig, on the northern shore of the Black Isle, became their main stronghold.

Other lands accrued over the centuries, including those of Braelangwell, Newhall, Meldrum, Byth, Craigston, Craighouse, and Kinbeachie, while it was at the beginning of the seventeenth century that John Urquhart of Craigfintray, known as the Tutor of Cromarty, built Craigston Castle, in Aberdeenshire.

William Urquhart, a grandson of Adam, the first hereditary sheriff of Cromarty, was rewarded for his family's efforts on behalf of the

Scottish Crown with the accolade of knighthood in 1416 from a grateful James I, while Thomas Urquhart was knighted by James VI in 1617.

By about the second half of the eighteenth century, however, the family had lost practically all of its lands, thus fulfilling a curious prophecy of the mysterious Coinneach Odhar ('dun-coloured Kenneth'), better known as the Seer of Kintail, or the Brahan Seer.

Born on the island of Lewis in the first half of the seventeenth century, but later settling in the Urquhart homelands, the Brahan Seer is reputed to have received the gift of Second Sight, or prophecy, in the form of a divining stone.

Burned for witchcraft at some stage between 1665 and 1675 at Chanonry Point, in Ross-shire, the seer is renowned today for a series of prophecies that have proved uncannily accurate.

These include the dramatic fall of the powerful House of Seaforth, the battle of Culloden of 1746 and the subsequent Highland Clearances, and 'horrid black rains' over the

Highlands that have been interpreted as referring to either the North Sea oil industry or, more alarmingly, nuclear fall-out.

The Brahan Seer is reputed to have told the laird of Urquhart, who may well have officiated at his execution in his capacity of sheriff, that 'the day is coming and is close at hand when the grasping Urquharts will not own above twenty acres of land in the shire of Cromarty.'

Although considered far-fetched at the time in view of the Urquharts' vast landholdings, the chilling prophecy has since proved accurate.

All that remains to the clan today is Craigston, in Aberdeenshire, owned by William Pratesi Urquhart, the ruins of Castle Craig on the Black Isle, and the ancient Cullicudden Old Kirkyard.

It was in 1959 that a Wilkins Urquhart, descended from Urquharts of Braelangswell who had immigrated to America in the eighteenth century, had his right officially established by the Lord Lyon King of Arms of Scotland as Chief of Clan Urquhart.

By that time Castle Craig had passed out of the family's possession, but it was gifted to the chief by Major Iain Shaw of Tordarroch 'as a unique symbol of amity between two great Highland clans.'

Castle Craig remains the seat of the clan chief, who at the time of writing is Kenneth Trist Urquhart of Urquhart, of Louisiana.

An Urquhart Clan Association flourishes today, promoting not only its own proud heritage and traditions in particular but that of Scotland in general.

There is also an official Urquhart clan tartan, while the stirring clan pipe music is 'When the Urquharts return to Glen Urquhart'.

Bearers of the surname of Cromarty, meanwhile, are recognised as a sept, or sub-branch, of the clan.

*Chapter three:*

# Jacobites and eccentrics

**A rather endearing strain of eccentricity appears to have flowed through the veins of a number of noted Urquharts, not least Thomas Urquhart of Cromarty, who died in 1557.**

In his twilight years it was his habit to order his long-suffering retainers to carry him from his castle on a couch every evening, and then laboriously hoist him up to the battlements through a complex system of pulleys.

This nightly ritual, he believed, was 'emblematical of the resurrection.'

He also appears to have been particularly virile, fathering no less than eleven daughters and twenty-five strapping sons – seven of whom fell defending their nation's freedom.

This was at the battle of Pinkie, fought on September 10, 1547 near Musselburgh, on Scotland's east coast, following the invasion of a 25,000-strong English army under the Duke of Somerset.

Three thousand clansmen and their kinsmen who fought under the leadership of the Earl of Argyll were either killed on the battlefield or forced to flee to safety.

The Urquharts proved unswerving in their support of the Royal House of Stuart, through all its various trials and tribulations, with the eccentric genius Sir Thomas Urquhart imprisoned for a time in the Tower of London for his loyalty to the ill-fated dynasty.

Born about 1611 in Cromarty, Sir Thomas is still famed for his celebrated translation of the work of the French satirist Francois Rabelais, in addition to a mathematical treatise published in 1645, a volume of epigrams, and his attempt to found a universal language.

Undoubtedly his most bizarre work, however, is the rather grandly titled *Pantochronachanon*, published in 1652, that traces the Urquharts' descent from Adam and Eve in the Garden of Eden!

During the bitter seventeenth century civil war between Crown and Covenant, Sir Thomas lent his support to Charles I and, following the king's execution, to his son, Charles II.

Scotland's nobles, barons, burgesses and ministers had signed a National Covenant that renounced Catholic belief, pledged to uphold the Presbyterian religion, and called for free parliaments and assemblies, at Edinburgh's Greyfriars Church on February 28, 1638.

Copies were made and dispatched around Scotland and signed by thousands more, making war with Charles I inevitable.

The first shots in this war were fired on May 14, 1639, in an action in which Sir Thomas Urquhart is believed to have taken part.

More of a skirmish than a battle, and known as the Trot of Turriff, it involved a force of Covenanters being forced to flee the Aberdeenshire village of Turriff when attacked by a determined band of Royalists.

Declared a traitor by the Scottish

Parliament, Sir Thomas, who had been knighted by Charles I himself, was later captured at the battle of Worcester, fought on September 3, 1651, when the forces of Oliver Cromwell soundly defeated Charles's successor, Charles II.

Pardoned by Cromwell about a year later and released from his captivity in the Tower of London, Sir Thomas returned for a time to Cromarty, only to depart for the Continent a short time afterwards.

It was here that he died in 1660 – reputedly from a fit of joyous and convulsive laughter after hearing of the Restoration of Charles II.

Nearly fifty-five years later, the Urquharts again proved loyal to the Stuart, or Jacobite, cause.

Opposition to the succession to the throne in 1714 of George, the Elector of Hanover, reached such a pitch that on September 6 of the following year the Jacobite Earl of Mar raised the Stuart Standard at Braemar.

He managed to muster a force of no less than 10,000 fighting men, who included both

Captain John Urquhart of Craigston and Colonel James Urquhart.

But the Jacobite cause was effectively lost after the battle of Sheriffmuir, in November of 1715, when Mar withdrew his forces north to Perth.

James VIII, known as the Old Pretender, landed at Peterhead from France in December, and then moved on to Perth, only to depart forever from Scottish shores in February of 1716.

The Rising had fizzled out, but the Stuart Standard was raised again more than thirty years later when James's son, Prince Charles Edward Stuart, arrived on Scottish shores.

Although the Urquharts played no active role in the disastrous battle of Culloden, fought on April 16, 1746, Colonel James Urquhart had performed the dangerous role of main Jacobite agent in Scotland until his death in 1741.

Following Culloden and the ending of all realistic hope of a Stuart restoration, Adam Urquhart of Blyth became a member of the prince's court-in-exile.

More than 150 years after Culloden, the Urquhart dynasty suffered a major blow when Major Beauchamp Urquhart, the last of the chiefly line (until Wilkins Urquhart was recognised as chief in 1959), was killed at the battle of Atbara, in the Sudan, in 1898.

The battle proved to be decisive in what was known as the Second Sudan War, with an Anglo-Egyptian force inflicting defeat on more than 6,000 Sudanese dervishes.

Major Urquhart fell as he led his troops of the Queen's Own Cameron Highlanders into battle, and his exploits were even recorded by the Dundee poet William Topaz McGonagall, who noted how his last words were reputed to have been 'never mind me my lads, fight on.'

On the battlefields of the twentieth century, Major General Robert Urquhart was the commander of the British 1st Airborne Division during Operation Market-Garden, in September 1945 – an audacious attempt to drive a sixty-mile salient into the German northern flank in Holland.

Urquhart lost three out of four of his men under withering fire in what proved to be the vicious and costly battle of Arnhem.

The action is depicted in the 1977 film *A Bridge Too Far*, with Sean Connery delivering a memorable performance as Major Urquhart.

*Chapter four:*

# Diplomacy and the arts

**Far from the field of battle, generations of Urquharts have achieved fame and distinction in a wide variety of pursuits.**

David Urquhart, born at Cromarty in 1805, was the diplomat and prolific writer who tirelessly campaigned for the Greek cause during the nation's war of independence with Turkey.

He was appointed to Britain's diplomatic mission to Constantinople in 1831, and it was here that he became enthralled with Turkey's ancient culture and civilisation.

An outspoken and controversial figure, he was recalled from his post in 1837, but later served as Member of Parliament for the English constituency of Stratford – proving to be a thorn in the flesh of successive government administrations.

Founder of the *Free Press* in 1855, which later as the *Diplomatic Review* had Karl Marx as one of its influential contributors, Urquhart was also responsible for the introduction of Turkish baths to Britain.

Also in the field of diplomacy, Sir Brian Urquhart, born in 1911, is the former Undersecretary-General of the United Nations who headed the organisation's peacekeeping efforts with great distinction from 1971 to 1986.

As the founder of UN peacekeeping operations, he is honoured today as one of the 'fathers' of peace keeping.

Thomas Urquhart, born in Canada in 1858 but whose father had emigrated from Dingwall, in Ross and Cromarty, in 1847, was the Mayor of Toronto for three successive terms, including in 1904, the year of the Great Toronto Fire.

In the world of music, Thomas Urquhart, who is believed to have been born in Scotland, was a London-based violin maker during the seventeenth century.

One of his precious violins, made in 1640, belongs to the accomplished contemporary violinist Karen Lack, who has performed with both the San Diego Symphony Orchestra and the Pacific Symphony Orchestra.

Craig Urquhart, meanwhile, is a distinguished American pianist and composer.

On the stage, Robert Urquhart, born in Ullapool, in Scotland in 1921, is the character actor and writer whose films include the 1985 *Restless Natives* and the 1981 *Dogs of War*.

Molly Urquhart, born in Glasgow in 1906, and who died in 1977, was the character actress who appeared in a number of films such as the 1950 *Clare*, and a number of popular television series such as *Dr Finlay's Casebook*.

In the heady realms of philosophy, British-born Alasdair Urquhart is the professor of philosophy at the University of Toronto who is widely acclaimed for his groundbreaking work in the field of logic.

In the world of literature, Jane Urquhart is the prolific Canadian poet and novelist born at Little Longlac, Ontario, in 1949, and whose works include *The Whirlpool*, *Away*, *The Stone Carvers*, and *A Map of Glass*.

Emma Urquhart, born in Inverness in 1991, holds the distinction of being one of the world's youngest authors.

Her first novel, *Dragon Towers*, was published at the tender age of thirteen, while a sequel, *Dragon Towers 2: Digital Tempest*, was published in 2005.